PRINCIPLES OF PROJECT PLANNING

COLLECTED WISDOM ON BUILDING
SOFTWARE

DON BURKS

ABOUT THE AUTHOR

Don Burks is Head Instructor of Lighthouse Labs, a software development bootcamp based in Vancouver, BC. Throughout his twenty year career in the world of IT and information services, Don has enjoyed some esteemed positions such as Senior Developer for MetroLyrics.com, Subject Matter Expert for MSN, Co-Founder and CTO of Nickler, Co-Founder and CTO of Pintellect, and CTO of LeftStuff (now StoryTap).

Originally dedicated to being a professional orchestral musician, Don holds a Bachelor of Musical Arts in Performance from Columbus State University in Columbus, Georgia. Born and raised in Atlanta, Georgia, Don now lives in Vancouver, BC. He is still an active musician, though his primary passion in recent years has been building digital literacy and passion for computational thinking and coding across Canada.

This is Don's second book, but first technical book and first e-book. In 2008, he published *Thirteen - Book One of the Crusader's Tale*, a fantasy novel that is the first of a two-book series. He is an active speaker, speaking at conferences and technical events around North America. He also writes a blog, hosted at https://donburks.com.

To reach out to the author:

https://donburks.com
don@donburks.com

ABOUT THIS BOOK

The book you are reading right now is the product of twenty years in the web and IT industry. It is the result of working on web sites, startups, mobile, desktop and web applications that have spanned a range of features, followings, and financials everywhere from fifty million unique visitors a month to a single pair of visitors in three months, and from a company that made over $100 million a year to a company that burned up $250k in just nine months. This book is the result of experience. This book is the result of making lots of mistakes, and seeing the mistakes of others. This book is based on lecture materials that were assembled to help aspiring developers taking an accelerated bootcamp program. Ultimately, this book is my way of writing down a solution to the colossal wasting of time and energy that I have seen people do when they have failed to plan their projects properly.

This book is about the principles of project planning, specifically building web and hybrid mobile applications. This book will present one strongly-spoken opinion on how to plan your project properly. The book you have started is packed with knowledge, wisdom, and insights that have been accumulated from working with developers

both great and horrible, from companies both amazing and medi-
ocre, and from a career that includes years of teaching, mentoring,
and studying the best practices of the web as well as being a front-
line developer building applications.

This book is opinionated, it is unapologetic, and it is guaranteed to
have content in it with which you will not agree. You will read
dogmatic proclamations, blanket statements voiced with absolute
certainty, and only an occasional hedging of opinion or offering of
compromise. You will find few equivocations. I'm pretty certain about
the topics and the approach, and in my experience the approach is
everything. More importantly, while this approach has worked for
me, the real proof is that I have seen others adopt this approach and
produce amazing software products.

This content is also known as The Sermon. Why is it referred to as a
sermon? Because every time I start talking about this, I get a little
preachy. I have strong opinions, and I also know that when it comes
to building quality products for the web, there are choices that must
be made, and planning that must be done. There is no acceptable
reason for not doing it properly. There are plenty of excuses, though.
In the bootcamp education space, students are used to hearing
teachers stand up and make strong statements about what is and is
not best practice. This particular lecture has stood out amongst
others, month after month and year after year, as being one of the
most opinionated ones that i give.

Overall, the biggest message of this book is that there are many
crucial things you need to think about before you put your fingers on
the keys. If you go through the planning that I recommend, your
product can succeed. I guarantee only that the method works and
produces working products. I cannot guarantee financial or critical
success. That's up to you, your team, and your ability to create a
product that resonates with customers. If you're looking for that, read
Malcolm Gladwell or Eric Ries, or listen to a Tim Ferriss podcast. If
you want to plan projects, keep reading.

WHO IS THIS BOOK FOR?

This book is written for less-experienced developers who have a product idea, and are probably going to end up working on it themselves. It is not written for product managers, unless you're a brand new PM and completely lost. It is written for coders who want to build something whole and complete, who are sure that their skill is sufficient to transform a back-of-the-napkin brainstorm into an app that will get *traction*, that fabled word that every product owner can't wait to hear or say.

This book is written for coders who have a hard drive full of half-finished side projects, a notebook full of pages of scribbled ideas that have never even gotten the treatment of setting up a boilerplate in an empty directory and then ignored for a few months or years. This book is written for you, someone who wants to build a great product, but has characteristically failed to follow through.

I have seen many developers struggle with the basic process of coming up with an idea and immediately jumping onto the keyboard, scaffolding up an app and starting to code. Inevitably, they get about thirty to fifty percent through the project and hit a roadblock. It's an obvious roadblock when they get to that point, but it was not so obvious when they had first sat down, full of hope and excitement. Sometimes, that roadblock means having to go back and re-build some part of their application. This is always a disheartening moment, because it means that you have to undo work. It means you've wasted time. And nothing kills productivity and momentum like wasting time.

This book is also for those developers who suffer from Impostor Syndrome (IS) about their apps. IS is a nasty little voice that lives in the back of our heads and tells us all sorts of discouraging things. It's the voice that tells you not to try for ambitious things, because they're too hard or because you're not skilled enough. It's the voice that tells you that you're a fraud when you're in a new situation, such as the first day of school or a new job. We all have that voice, it's our built-in fight-or-flight mechanism kicking in and trying to get us to get out of an uncomfortable situation by psyching us out. That voice is loud, insistent, and doesn't like hard work. It definitely is the reason gym memberships that start right after New Year's tend to be dropped by the middle of February. It's the reason relationships fail early on, and definitely what causes twenty-something adults to move back in with their parents when the real world gets rough.

When you're building an app, and having the hubris to presume that you can just craft something great out of nothing, IS will rear its ugly head. But, this is where my book can help you. If you've planned properly, and followed the principles outlined here, then you are assured to be able to stare IS in the face and tell it to shut up. Whenever that voice kicks in, usually when a problem arises, write one more line of code. If you can write one more line of code, then you have proven that voice wrong. And if that voice is wrong about that moment, then it is wrong about everything.

THE IDEA

Every app starts as an idea. Maybe it was a dream, maybe it was a daydream. Perhaps you were using one application and wished it did something specific that it doesn't, and realized you could build something that filled that need. Maybe you were doodling and that inspired an idea. Perhaps it was an assignment, or a hackathon, or a case study you read in a book. Regardless of where it came from, you now have this idea that is running around the inside of your head and demanding attention. These situations are great, because they seem to come from nowhere and they energize us like a lightning bolt.

So, now that you have come up with an idea, you start thinking about its potential. You think that you have come up with a great way to sell something to people, to make some money. Perhaps you believe you have a solution to enact change, to make the world a better place. A product that, once put into the hands of users, is going to work. People will be amazed, astounded, blown away. They'll want to use it again and again. You will change the world if only you can get this thing built.

Fortunately, you are a developer. You solve problems with code. You have studied syntax, logic, data, and esoteric concepts such as REST, CRUD, BREAD, ACID, and a number of other acronyms. You cannot wait to get your fingers on the keys, to write code that is going to render whatever perceived opportunity for billion-dollar revenue or sweeping social change that you may have dreamed up. Code is the toolkit with which you have conquered the world so far and is the one you are going to reach for to make this new vision come to life.

But something you have to realize is that in order to make your app work, it's not about the code. You likely work for someone in a developer role, going in to work every day to churn out subroutines and make unit tests pass. And I'm going to start off by telling you something terribly controversial.

No one hires you to code.

No developer studio, no technical manager, no HR office, no CEO, and certainly no company is ever going to hire you to code. In every case, you are being hired to build and/or maintain a product. Yes, you will likely write code to build and/or maintain that product, but as a point of fact the purpose for bringing you on as a developer is for product. This is a truth of the development world, and one that will change your viewpoint about your role, once you realize it. If it's something that you haven't thought about before, go think about it. I'll wait.

All good now? Great. So, no one hires you to code. But you want to build a product. This might even turn into a company one day. This product might have tens of thousands of users. It will have all kinds of great features. It will use all sorts of really cool technologies, all the cutting edge things you've read about on Hacker News and Reddit.

Where do you start? Well, that's a great question. And unfortunately, in your IDE or text editor is not the right answer. What I want you to embrace is the idea that you have a fair amount of work to do *before* you start writing code, so that when you do get your itchy little fingers on the keyboard you will have a clear picture of exactly what it is you're going to be building. Far too often, I have seen developers make the mistake of diving right into the code without a clear idea of what the code is supposed to do, and it quickly turns into spaghetti that neither can be used, or launched. And that code inevitably isn't something which the developer wants to take either credit or blame for in the marketplace.

You have to realize that the difference between credit and blame is success. And in the world of technology, success comes from you contributing something to the world, not just consuming. Sure, you want to use that cool library, or you want to build that killer app, but you need to make sure you are contributing something worthwhile.

That being said, don't be scared of presenting an idea that has already been done before. Derivative is good. Derivative is where innovation really happens. Twitter is just SMS messages for the web. Instagram is a photo album that digitally records when Aunt Ethel says she likes that photo, or comments that you look fat in those shorts. LinkedIn is a digital Rolodex, and Amazon is the comprehensive digital catalogue of goods that Sears & Roebuck always dreamed of being.

Differentiation, extension, enhancement, specialization, and internationalization are all ways in which you can make your product stand out from everything else that may be out there on the market. Just because you haven't succeeded yet doesn't mean you won't. Your idea has merit. You just need to change your approach.

What NOT to build

There are a few ideas that I hope you're not doing. Please, for the sake of all of the tech world, please stop building bar-finders and dating apps. *But the bars are recommended by my friends!* you exclaim. It's still a bar finder. *But I'm getting fitness enthusiasts to run together!* you insist. It's just a dating app. Oh, and please stop building that app where you list the ingredients of your fridge and it gives you a recipe. It's been done. It's overdone. Please, for the love of whatever you consider holy, stop. Go look at Product Hunt, or a similar marketplace for new SaaS products. Look at the new releases on the app store for your mobile platform. If you are seeing ten variants of the same product you intend to build, then you need to ask yourself if your version of it is worth pursuing, or whether you need to find a new, more unique idea. At the end of the day, if you decide that you're doing to make an app that matches you up with other people who only have mayo and leftover spring rolls in their fridge at a nearby bar so that you can both go exercise, then go build it. But do a good job with it, please.

Do not rely on friends and family for input

Likely, your idea is a great idea. Just ask you, you'll tell us. But you're biased, so you go to friends and family. Even the taxi driver and the bartender have been consulted, and they all liked it. In fact, everyone that you've talked to about it has said that it's the greatest idea they've ever heard. They can't wait for you to build it, and they are sure to sign up. This is honestly meaningless feedback. And it is the worst sort of feedback that you can get. People, by nature, do not want to do anything that would be perceived as discouraging ambition. So you will always hear positive feedback, and it won't help you to move your product forward. There may be a few friends you can count on to give you their honest opinion, to play the proverbial Devil's Advocate. You're more likely to get an honest opinion from strangers on the street or in a coffee shop than you are from your immediate circle of friends, family, or even co-workers.

Until you can present an idea to someone that is going to inspire them to give you money for it, right there on the spot, you want to refine your pitch. Until you have gotten $20 from them, they haven't done anything to support you. More importantly, you haven't validated your idea. And this is critical. You have to validate your idea as being something that people are willing to invest time and money into, because they see how it is going to benefit them. Otherwise, you're just getting feedback that benefits you. Friends and family love you and want to see you succeed. The taxi driver wants a good tip. Even if your idea is the worst thing they have ever heard, they are not likely to tell you. They will encourage you and push you to build it, because it seems to be making you happy.

Describing your idea to others

When you pitch your idea, you probably start the pitch the same way, every time. It likely sounds something like:

"Wouldn't it be cool if there was an app that _____?"

Or the other popular version:

"I'm going to build _____ for _____."

Maybe your idea is an ice cream truck popsicle cost comparison tool, maybe your app is tracking water quality in underdeveloped parts of the world. Perhaps you want a real-time dashboard of your fantasy sports scores or an app that decides how you're feeling by analyzing the sentiment of the lyrics in the songs on your playlist. These and ten thousand more ideas come up every day. What matters is what your idea actually represents.

You have identified a problem. That problem could be one that doesn't have a current solution, it could also be a problem for which there are many solutions. But there may not be a solution that solves the problem in exactly the way you are proposing. In every case, though, whether you have asked if it would be cool if an app existed, or pitched Tinder for Cats, you are actually stating a fundamental proposition:

"If I had access to a particular set of data, I could present it in a way that adds value."

DATA

You're not ready to code, yet. First, we have to learn about data.

Your data is your product. This is an absolute of the technical world. When you come up with your idea, you state with confidence that if you had access to a particular set of data, you could present it in a valuable way. Your data is going to be the most important thing which you manage. Whether your product is for the purpose of acquiring the data you need to demonstrate the value, or whether your product is going to acquire data from some external source such as an API, that data is your product.

Let's consider a social media monolith, Tweetbookagram, for a moment. The go-to platform for pokes and cat gifs and mis-attributed quotes, we consume vast stores of data from that service. However, many people would consider the website or the mobile app to be the Tweetbookagram product. To disprove this, I have to lead you through a bit of a thought experiment.

Let's assume that the world is exactly as we know it to be now, with the addition of one malicious, mischievous wizard. This wizard *hates* Tweetbookagram. This wizard will wave his magic wand and the website and the mobile app for Tweetbookagram will be eradicated from the universe. All the backups, all installations, they are all gone.

Now, on the one hand, productivity around the world goes up 20%. Tweetbookagram's stock might drop a proportional amount. However, the legions of developers that work there put their heads together, and rebuild the app and the site. A few weeks go by, and we're back to inviting our friends to chase candy across a screen for pixelated coins, and chuckling nervously about that time we couldn't hit our news feed for a few days.

Tweetbookagram as we know it survives, and thanks to the marketing department recovering from the heart attack that the wizard gave them, is being pitched as better than ever. Signups go up, stock prices go up, and all is right with the world.

But let's take that same little wizard and have him wave his magic wand again. He's not going to be deterred, and if anything, he's madder than ever before. The database of Tweetbookagram disappears. All the backups vanish in a puff of smoke. You go to log in to your social media and there is no account. You were concerned because you stopped getting notifications. All the pictures, the events, the comments from friends and enemies alike are gone. A few people might sign back up, and all of the buzz on the local news will be about how much of a tragedy it is.

However, this time Tweetbookagram as we know it is dead and gone. What made it valuable was the aggregate of all the data it had stored. The value that it gave to its users was giving them access to that data. Years and years of users plugging their lives into the platform meant that all of the features that the developers had built all gave value because there was a benefit to that presentation of that data. Without the data, the benefit to the users was gone.

When you are starting to plan out a project, you definitely want to start with planning your data. When you are starting, I suggest asking yourself three very important questions:

1. **What data can I access or acquire?** - This is a very important question! Is there an API that can give you the data you need? Can you get users to input it? Can it be scraped, parsed, or extrapolated from somewhere? This is the root source of your data, and is the most important question you are going to answer about your product.

2. **Can I correlate that data to something else?** - Raw data, by itself, isn't very interesting. Data doesn't have to be ugly, but plain data by itself isn't particularly stimulating for the average user. What makes data interesting is our ability to correlate it to something else. Showing a connection between things often demonstrates a heretofore unknown association or trend. Most successful apps are not about a single series of data; there is almost always a correlation.

3. **How do I pivot the correlation to provide value?** - Fantastic, you have a source of data, you've correlated it to something else, but now you need to present it in a compelling way. What is the mechanic you are going to use to pivot your data and demonstrate why your product is the best way to access that data?

Once you have answered these three questions, you are ready to understand the value that your app brings. You are ready to clearly and articulately express the benefit that your users will get out of your presentation of data.

FEATURES VS. BENEFITS

You're still not ready to code. Be patient, we have to figure out why we're going to code what we will code, when it is time.

As any marketing person will probably tell you, users don't pay for features. And when I say pay, I don't mean just money. I also mean time and effort. Time is money, in the immortal words of Benjamin Franklin. Effort takes time, as well, so at the end of the day we are talking about the user spending something that is of value to them to use your solution. Encouragement and kind words are free, as we discussed earlier. It's the $20 of time or money that you are chasing. Ultimately, you want to present a product that someone is willing to invest themselves in. You want to change their mind about using something new, and make it worth their while to change their daily or weekly habits to include the use of your application.

What a user **will** pay for is a benefit. Something that benefits them and makes them feel like there is a justifiable reason for them to use a product. People don't pick products because of a smooth transition on a drop-down menu. They don't pick a product because it autocompletes their searches. They don't choose to spend their time and energy because of the way an app uploads a file. Gradients on buttons never made users sign up for subscriptions.

Users always pick a product because the particular presentation of the data that the creators of that product have given them benefits them and enriches their experience in some way. Exclusively, this happens when a feature is able to service one of the **Universal Values.**

Universal Values

There are four basic motivations that humans have for making decisions. And as developers, we speak to these four motivations all the time. The features we deliver address these Universal Values by demonstrating benefit to a user in one of four key areas. Every decision we make, whether it is the shoes we wear, the food we eat, the people we date, or the music we listen to is driven by at least one of these four values.

1. **Look good** - We love to look good to others. We want other people to think that we make good choices, that we are good people. We want to be viewed as smart, attractive, formidable, desirable, wise, and accomplished. This is a fundamental drive that everyone has.
2. **Feel good** - This is an internal view on ourselves. The same way that we want people to think that we make good choices, we want to feel good about the choices we make. Conspicuously, we may make choices to make other people like us even though we don't feel good about those choices ourselves. And we usually label *integrity* as someone who makes choices that make them feel good about what they have chosen even if others disagree.
3. **Save time** - Time is the one resource that we do not know how much we have. There is no way to tell when our time is up. At any given moment, an errant rock or a disease or a chance encounter with a blimp may end our lives and there

is often very little we can do about it. Therefore, we do our best to conserve our time and imbue as much value into the moments we do get to enjoy as we can.

4. **Save money** - We work hard to acquire our resources. The money in our bank accounts, the nice car in the garage, the boats and purses and jewelry that mark our accomplishments in the world. Even if you are not materialistic, you recognize that resources are finite and must be conserved. As such, there is a universal motivation to preserve the resources to which you have attached value.

With these values in mind, you are able to shape the focus of your product and refine how you are presenting your data. If your product isn't addressing at least one of these values, then it is destined to fail. However, if you can conceive of a presentation of data that is going to touch on multiple members of the **Universal Values**, you have a powerful product indeed.

USER SPECIFICATIONS

Definitely not ready to code yet. More planning to do.

Going as far back as the turn of the 21st century, a mechanism called *user stories* has been used to help software developers quantify and qualify the core interactions that an end user will have with a product. User stories are a mechanism that grew out of the Extreme Programming (XP) movement, and have morphed over the years into their place in the Agile ecosystem.

They are also an extremely useful tool which gives you a deep insight into the reasoning behind why a user might choose to engage with a feature. User stories can be written in the positive and the negative and when used to help quantify a list of features to be delivered in a sprint or as part of an MVP.

A basic user story takes the format:

"As a _____,

I want to _____,

Because _____."

Typically, the blanks are represented in the following manner:

"As a <role>,

I want to <action>,

Because <positive outcome>."

These are outstanding models of describing an end-user's interaction with a site. Here are some examples of how you might fill them out:

Role	Action	Outcome
As a user	I want to view cat gifs	Because they make me happy
As an admin	I want to reset a user's password	Because I want them to be able to access their account.
As a guest	I want to learn about new features	Because I may want to sign up

Another variation on the classic user story is:

"As a <role>,

I should be able to <action>,

Because <positive outcome>."

Of course, user stories can also be expressed in the negative, such as:

"As a <role>,

I don't want to <action>,

Because <positive outcome>."

And:

"As a <role>,

I should not be able to <action>,

Because <positive outcome>."

The "because" is very important to the user story, because it speaks to the specific benefit which the user is going to get from the interaction. If you can't think of a "because" for a particular feature, you have to ask yourself the question, 'Do I need to build it at all?' The answer is almost definitely going to be 'No'.

User Scenarios

Just as a User Story is going to describe the motivation behind a particular feature, a User Scenario is going to describe the actual mechanic and situation in which a feature is experienced. These are also called Acceptance Tests in some contexts, but there are a lot of definitions for that term. The model I am going to propose is the Given-When-Then model as described as part of the Agile Manifesto. This model describes how an action will resolve, given a particular context. It follows this format:

"Given <some context>,

When <some action is taken>,

Then <some outcome occurs>."

For example:

"Given that I am logged out,

When I enter my credentials and submit the login form,

Then I am logged into the site."

Another example:

"Given that I am on my account summary page,

When I pay a bill using this account,

Then I should see the available balance lower by the corresponding amount."

In my experience, this model can be extended by adding an 'And' clause which can help indicate the change in UI/UX as a result of the action taken. Here is an example of the 'And' clause being implemented:

"Given <some context>,

When <some action is taken>,

Then <some outcome occurs>,

And <some visible result is seen>."

A real-world example would be:

"Given that I am looking at my inbox,

When I receive a new e-mail,

Then I should see it at the top of my inbox,

And the unread count should increment by 1."

User Specifications

Thanks to a November 2014 article by Jon Dobrowolski titled 'A *Framework for Modern User Stories*', I have been a tremendous fan of building out far more rich user specifications that combine User Stories and User Scenarios. By combining these two descriptions of an end-user's interaction, and adding some metadata, you end up with a full specification for a feature that you want to build into your application.

In that spirit, here is the structure of a full User Specification:

"As a <role>,

I want to <action>,

Because <positive outcome>.

Given <some context>,

When <some action is taken>,

Then <some outcome occurs>,

And <some visible result is seen>."

INFO:

<Metadata about spec here>

Here is a User Specification filled out for an export option for a word processor: ∕

"As a document author,

I want to export my document as a PDF,

Because I want to distribute it in multiple formats.

Given that I am currently editing the document,

When I click the export button,

Then the app prompts me to save the PDF file,

And I can see the exported file in my filesystem."

INFO:

Export button: /assets/img/export_btn.png

User Specs are incredibly important, and will serve as the blueprints and foundation of many of the other principles of project planning that will be covered in this book. We'll keep coming back to these, because there is a ton of information that you can glean from them. It is heavily recommended to write out User Specs for all of the features that you want to build. Whether you are building a proof-of-concept, a basic MVP, or a full enterprise application, you will (or should) know what the core level of functionality is that you need to ship when the project is first launched and deployed. No piece of software is ever done. However, that doesn't mean that you can't quantify the specific list of abilities that end-users will have when they are inter-acting with your app. Whether that is Phase 1 of a launch, or six years afterwards, when you are releasing a new feature, you should have the ability to verbalize why the user wants to use it, and what the general workflow will be.

Negative Specs

It is entirely possible to write out specifications that highlight a negative condition. These can be very important to help write unit tests or TDD/BDD testing in support of the features that you are delivering to your users. In these cases, you might use one of these types of assertions:

"As a <role>,

I do NOT want to <action>,

Because <negative effect>"

OR:

"As a <role>,

I should NOT be able to <action>,

Because <negative outcome>"

These can be extremely useful to you as the application developer, as this may deal with issues of authorization or access to resources.

FEATURE COMPLETE

Still not ready to code. Be patient.

You, as the product owner, decide what "Feature Complete" means. When your product, or your next release rolls out the door, you decide what the full set of features must be to make that release valuable. You want to make sure you are shipping the features that your users will need to effectively use the product. Features should not be frivolous, and should all impart value, as determined by User Specs.

When defining "Feature Complete," you have to realize that it does not mean what the software *could* do given an infinite budget and an infinite amount of time. As a general rule, when working with a team and brainstorming about the capabilities that you intend to ship, the phrase "Wouldn't it be cool if..." is banned from the room. It is great when you are ideating at the beginning, before you have User Specs. However, when you are coming up with the specific list of features that you're going to deliver, it is deadly. Yes, it **would** be cool if you could build all sorts of great things. You have to learn to translate 'Wouldn't it be cool if...' into 'While it would be great if...'. Come to the planning with the mindset of "It **will** be cool when we build X." Make sure that each and every feature that you intend to build is justified by the benefit it's going to bring your user, and because it validates the core set of features that your product delivers.

There is a trap though. The trap is that developers tend to over-promise and under-deliver. Developers love to play with new technologies, refactor to eliminate technical debt, and try out new ideas. And none of these are bad things, but unfortunately deadlines also matter, and in all three of these situations the developer doesn't know what they don't know. The discovery of those absences of knowledge or skill are often deadly to being able to ship. Pick a deadline, define a set of features that will be delivered, and stick to that as much as possible. It takes discipline not to be seduced by the clarion call of 'But there's this new library....'.

One last tip that is worth mentioning, particularly if you are doing work for someone else and using this set of planning steps as a guide, is that you should never take on work that you don't have time to deliver properly. Whether the deadline is externally set or internally given, never work without enough time to do your best work. You will never be satisfied with your efforts, and most likely your clients and users won't be either. You'll always be let down, and that is not the kind of developer you want to be.

Winchester Mansion

The former residence of Sarah Winchester, in San Jose, California is the perfect example of the "Wouldn't it be cool if" mentality. Built using the fortune inherited by Sarah from her late husband Sam, of

Winchester rifle fame, it was built as a coping mechanism for Sarah's mental and emotional issues. She believed that she was haunted by the ghosts of people killed by her husband's rifles, and that her dead husband had spoken to her through a medium instructing her to continuously build a house to fool the ghosts.

Stairways go into the ceiling, windows look onto other rooms, of the dozens of bathrooms in the house only one worked. The rest were decoys, since the ghosts traveled through the plumbing. Of course. The house was continually added onto with no plans, no architect, no rhyme or reason. There was no plan.

You're probably asking yourself why I am taking the time in a book about building software to talk about a crazy woman's house in southern California. There is a very good reason. It is all too common that I see younger developers get pulled this way and that by ideas, or worse, by other people. Startups that could have launched in two or three months take two years to get something public, because there's a constant need to build "just one more feature" in, to land a big client. Avoid this instinct.

Don't let your app be a Winchester mansion!

Ship a product

Software is never done. We know this. We know that there can always be one more feature, one more bugfix, one more CSS or layout tweak. You can always do A/B testing, resolve technical debt, clean up and refactor the code base. This infinite ability to extend, improve, and expand a project's scope puts developers and product owners in an interesting position. There is an almost unanswerable question, namely 'When is it ready to ship?' The game 'Duke Nukem Forever' was famously delayed in its release, with the dev team always answering the question of when it would ship with the statement 'When it is done.'

It would be easy to procrastinate forever and always give yourself a bit more time to "brush up" the UI or tangle with that one edge case that was never quite handled in development. However, that isn't feasible in most cases. In most cases, the dev team is going to be under pressure from the business team to ship the product, get it out the door. There will be dire predictions about lost customers, dwindling revenues, some vague reference to having to eat ramen for a month.

If this is a side project, or if your mortgage and grocery bill are not dependent on your ability to ship this code, then you actually will have a harder job of deciding when you're going to call your code 'shippable'. Regardless of whether the deadline is financially real or arbitrary, the mentality needs to stay the same. There needs to be a deadline by which the core features you have decided upon building (based on your user stories) will be working.

Regardless, for the purpose of this book, we are going to consider a few glossary terms to talk about the state of code when it ends up in front of end users.

- **Testable** - An implementation of a feature which the dev team believes solves the problem, but needs to be tested to verify and validate.
- **Shippable** - Tested code that works and executes the feature as designed.
- **Finished** - Shippable code that has been reviewed, refactored, and revised until it is the best implementation which the current team can deliver, given all factors.

Testing

It's worth taking some time to talk about testing. To discuss testing, we need to discuss a real-world example. Let's say you hear about a new thing, a flying car. Recently invented, all the latest fashion, you decide you're going to try one out. You find a company that will rent one to you, you settle yourself down into the driver's seat and study the controls. Great labeling, a good user experience, and some intu-ition allow you to confidently place your hands on the controls and begin to use it.

But was it tested? You don't know, but you would hope so. Wouldn't you? The ability to fly, to stop, to land, these were all features of the machine that were tested. Right? You could assure yourself that they wouldn't have released it for public use if it wasn't tested.

Parachutes, zip lines, anti-lock brakes, pharmaceuticals, pre-pack-aged pizza, and life rafts all are examples of products that we would probably use blindly without giving thought to whether all of the aspects of them were tested adequately. We would have the assured ignorance that they wouldn't be on consumer shelves or available for private use if they weren't tested. But we don't have the same arro-gance about software. SaaS products enter the market every day, apps pop up in our app marketplaces by the dozens, and never once do we concern ourselves with their tests.

We put our credit cards, our children's birthdays, our personally-identifying information into these apps without a single thought about whether the apps have been tested for proper behaviour. Is there a moral to this cautionary section? Of course.

Test your code. There is no excuse not to do it.

I have seen plenty of business and management leaders direct devel-opers not to do any software testing. Developers want to ensure that code behaves as desired. There is nothing worse than saying some-thing is done, having someone sit down in front of it and test an edge case that the dev hadn't thought of and breaking the feature. Some-times, simply choosing to do actions in a particular order can cause undesired effects. The executives or managers that make these deci-sions aren't feeling malicious towards the developers, and they definitely are not trying to doom their product. What they are worried about is the cost of development time. Every day the app or a feature isn't in the marketplace is a day that revenue cannot be made.

Managers may settle for testing based on usage after development as a litmus test for whether the work is complete. Developers may have suggested doing TDD or BDD approaches and been shot down as costing too much to build the test suites out. I have seen (and been in) situations where even unit testing after the fact was vetoed due to budgetary reasons. All of these are regrettable scenarios. But ultimately, there is no excuse for not doing software testing.

Test your code. There is no one "best" way to test your code. TDD and BDD have their benefits, unit testing gives you a clear finish line. Implementation testing, regression testing, usability testing, these are all valuable parts of the process and each can and will reveal their own deficiencies. Just do it, as the sports footwear company tells us.

CAPTURING THE A-HA MOMENT

No coding yet. You've got time. Breathe.

There is a moment for every user, when viewing a great product for the first time, where the implementation of a particular feature or combination of features gives them a realization that the product in question offers something unique. That thrill, that tipping point where a product goes from something that you are just trying out to something you could see integrating into your everyday life, is what I call the A-Ha moment.

As a developer, as a contributor to product, as someone whose keystrokes have contributed to hundreds of applications, I can assure you that you will learn to live for that moment. That is what you are working for. Even if you have built your app for just yourself, when it does what you need it to do and offers a solution to the problem that prompted you to build it in the first place, that accomplishment is real. There is a famous quote:

"I do not think there is any thrill that can go through the human heart like that felt by the inventor as he sees some creation of the brain unfolding to success... such emotions make a man forget food, sleep, friends, love, everything."

- Nikola Tesla

When you are still at the stage of development where you are looking at a collection of user specifications and deciding what you want to deliver, pick a feature or related set of features, and put a star on that selection. These are your A-Ha Moment features that you are making a contract with yourself to deliver. These are going to be the metaphorical hook that sets into the mouth of your users, as it would were you fishing.

DEPLOYMENT

Not ready to code yet. We need to make some technical decisions first.

One of the things I recommend to decide on before you even get to the point of designing is to make some solid decisions about how you are going to deploy your project. The reason I recommend making these decisions at such an early, pre-coding stage is that this decision will potentially impact a number of your other technology choices that you will make along the way.

As well, this can be a decision that directly impacts your branding. Since we are focusing on building a product, not just coding some pretty algorithms, the branding and identity of our product is incredibly important. One of the most important deployment decisions you can make is to ask yourself the question:

"Am I going to buy a domain name for this product?"

Domain Names

The decision to buy a domain name is one that some people agonize over, and others treat with a very laissez-faire attitude. You want a good domain, but you don't want to pay a lot for it. What is the right extension to use? What is the right registrar, the right hosting? Buying a domain isn't just picking a name for your app. It is its address, the first and most recognizable way that users will access your product.

It is worth noting at this point that domain names carry with them a few responsibilities that you will need to figure out if you are not already familiar with configuring and maintaining them. The first is that you will need to become familiar with nameservers, which are the mechanism by which the internet knows that your domain points to an IP address. You will set these up with your registrar to point to the IP address of wherever you are hosting the app. This is why the decisions about deployment are important to make ahead of time. Without knowing where you are going to be hosting your app, you can't configure your domain name correctly.

As well, please keep in mind that by buying a domain name, you are obligating yourself to that name for a minimum of one year. It's not to say that you can't buy a different domain and re-brand, but registrations for domains are on a year-by-year basis. So if you typo your domain name, congratulations! You own a misspelled domain for a year.

Hosting

There are many, many options for hosting your app. Some of them are influenced by cost, some are by availability, some are chosen for legal reasons, and others are based on features that are needed. Some of the more popular options include services like Amazon Web Services, Microsoft Azure, Digital Ocean, Heroku, Linode, and Joyent. Depending on the technical stack you intend to use, your hosting choices may be limited.

Conversely, depending on the hosting choices you make, your tech stack may be limited. Some services like AWS and Heroku, for instance, will charge extra for each additional instance or service (such as MongoDB) that you need. Others such as Digital Ocean or Linode are far more open-ended, but will require that you do more manual configuration.

Additionally, your hosting choices will imply a certain level of system administration or DevOps work in addition to the coding of your project. This **must** be factored into your time management. There will be time needed for setting up the server with whatever hosting service you are using, making sure dependencies get installed, making sure that your runtime environments are at the right version. There may be networking that has to be configured, file permissions. You also have to consider **how** you are going to deploy your app. Are you going to use git to deploy, a service such as CircleCI or Travis/Jenkins, or just old-school file transfers?

These are all considerations that you need to have planned out ahead of time. These are not decisions you want to be making the day before your app is supposed to go live. At that point, you don't know what you don't know, and therefore cannot scope out your schedule and task/time management properly. As well, if you don't have previous experience with DevOps work, the learning curve will seem to be much steeper as a result of the need to make a looming deadline.

Deployment Gotchas

One of the most common mistakes I see when web developers are deploying their projects is a failure to take into consideration some of the assumptions they had made when developing locally. I will list these here under 'Networking Considerations' because they are almost always connected to resources that you access over the network.

1. **CORS** - Cross-Origin Resource Sharing needs to be enabled if you are retrieving data from somewhere other than the

SOP(Same Origin Policy) allows. If you don't know what any of these terms means and you're using or planning to use AJAX, then you need to do some research.

2. **Absolute URLs** - Have you hardcoded URLs into your project? If so, you should probably either find a way to make them relative, or make them configurable with environment variables. Hardcoding URLs is **not** a best practice.

3. **Upload availability** - Do you have a feature that allows users to upload resources to the server? Do you plan on scaling your app across multiple servers? How are you going to guarantee upload availability? (See #2 as well for this) Have you considered using a CDN service?

4. **Propagation** - If you are pointing your domain name to a new nameserver, have you allowed ample time for TTLs(Time To Live) to expire before you are announcing your launch?

DATABASE

Unfortunately, you're still not ready to code.

Since, as we have already established, your data is your product, then one of the most important technical decisions you can make is how you store your data. Which database engine are you intending to use? You're not ready to code, but you do need to start making some technical decisions. Hosting was the first decision you made about your tech stack. This is going to be the second. And this one is a good one to make here, because it could conceivably influence a number of other decisions you might make later on, such as sharding, ORM choice, or mobile synchronization.

Relational Databases

Traditional rows and columns, SQL as your query language, this is the mainstay of web development. Relational databases are stable, consistent, reliable, and built to make the rapid storage and retrieval of information an easy task.

NoSQL Database

Document storage, almost always stored in JSON format, these databases are useful when you have a smaller number of data models, or data models that are tightly associated with each other. Typically, NoSQL databases trade off consuming lots of disk space for having a rich and very elaborate level of indexing which makes searching faster than traditional SQL databases.

Single vs. Multi-user databases

If you're building a mobile app but need the structure of a relational database, you may find yourself reaching for SQLite or an in-memory database such as PouchDB. Make sure that if you are choosing one of these, or if you are using it for local development work instead of production use, that you are comfortable with the number of users and the amount of data they can hold before they become impractical.

DbAAS

It is worth calling out here that you may want to use something like DynamoDB, Firebase, ParseServer, or Couchbase as an online data store. These are almost always HTTP-based APIs that have a particular query structure that is not the same as you would have with either SQL or NoSQL syntaxes. They can be very useful for MVP or proof-of-concept coding, but aren't going to necessarily scale up to an enterprise level. Make sure you do your due diligence ahead of time, as there are often query limit thresholds that can trigger costs you may not be prepared for.

Principles of picking a DB

Overall, the guiding principle you want to use is this:

Store your data the way you intend to query your data.

If you intend to request large, data-rich documents of key-value data, then use a document database such as Mongo or Couch. If you intend to query your data where you are looking for data relationships above and beyond just what a relational foreign-key relationship would give, maybe you want a graph database like Neo4j.

Perhaps you want high-throughput key-value storage, so you go for something like Redis. Maybe you are dealing with gargantuan big data sets where you will be querying millions of rows at a time, so you may want to go for something like Hadoop or Cassandra.

If you're going to be querying data models with clear one-to-many relationships, then you should absolutely be choosing a relational database of some SQL flavour. Now, as far as whether to choose MySQL, PostgreSQL, MariaDB, Percona, or some other flavour... just pick Postgres and be done with it. <opinion>It's the best combo of performance and power you're going to get in this realm.</opinion>

More than many other technical decisions, I advocate for you to decide on this early, as once you go down one path it becomes very taxing to have to change your database, especially if you start with document/NoSQL and have to change to SQL. Be smart and make good decisions up front to save yourself the stress and time investment later on.

ERD

Unfortunately, you're not ready to code yet. You need to design your data first. The initialism ERD stands for **E**ntity **R**elationship **D**iagram, and it is the tool that software developers use to design and visualize both the schema and the interconnectedness of their data. The structure of your data, meaning the fields, types, tables/collections, and relationships within your data, is one of the single most important things you can plan before starting to code your app.

An ERD is a critical piece of planning, because it allows you to plan for what data you initially believe you need to collect. And, as previously stated, your data **IS** your product. It only makes sense that if your data is your product, then the design and structure of your data is an initial skeleton of the structure of your application. This is where you get to model out the data you plan to collect, and associate it with the appropriate table or collection. As stated in the previous section talking about databases, there is a single guiding principle that you want to pursue here.

Store your data the way you intend to query your data.

Think about what the major 'nouns' of your application are. A great way to do that is to look at your user specification. You remember your user specifications, right? Full of nouns. Consider the following user spec, with nouns bolded:

As a **user**,

I want to search for **stories** that I find interesting,

Because I like new content.

Given that I am on the search page,

When I enter a **keyword** to search for,

I get a listing of **stories** that match,

And I can click on a **story** to read it.

Given that spec, it's clear that if we are using SQL, we need three tables: users, stories, and keywords. It's also clear that we are going to need to have an association between stories and keywords, so that implies a join table of some sort. This is probably a scenario where instead of building a keywords_stories table, we can add some metadata and create a tags table that represents the unique combination of a keyword and a story. This also informs where our Foreign Key assignments are going to be, and helps us to determine if any of them are cascades.

If this was NoSQL, we would probably have User and Story as collections, and know that an individual Story in a collection is probably going to have keywords as a key, potentially containing nested documents.

In planning out a table, or a collection, we can make some determinations about what data points we intend to collect. Our aforementioned user is probably going to have a username, a display name, an e-mail address, a password digest, a boolean field for whether they are an admin (or maybe an integer or char field for an ACL role). We may want to track things like last login, phone number, or maybe some other marketing or CRM-related information such as whether they receive the newsletter, depending on our application. Given these fields, we can determine if a SQL table needs an index on any fields (I'd suggest the admin/acl field and the newsletter field, for example).

Whatever schema we generate in our ERD is not permanent. As we are talking about project planning, this is an INITIAL sketch of what data you plan to collect. Many developers I have seen get very attached to their schemas, treating them as if they were engraved in stone tablets and cannot be changed. Not only do most languages, frameworks, and ORMs include the concept of data migrations, but again this is only the planning stage of your app. This tells you where you are starting from, and I have seen many developers turn their ERD into an organic, living document that evolves alongside the app as their development progresses.

When building an ERD, this is a great time to engage all of the stakeholders to make sure all of their needs are initially planned out in the data design. Also include all levels of your development team, as everyone should feel a sense of ownership and contribution to this process. The data models underpin everything that you are going to build, and it only makes sense that everyone who is going to be affected by the decisions you make here is consulted.

TECHNICAL ARCHITECTURE

We need to decide what we are going to code with, before we can code. Let's do that now, because you're still not ready to code.

Unless you are building apps like a self-contained mobile app, an API-consuming single page web application, or a desktop editor app, you are probably going to need to build a server application that can serve up data and state for your product. Even though you're not ready to start coding on that server app yet, you do need to make some strong decisions now about what language you're going to be using and whether you need particular libraries or frameworks to deliver your core value proposition.

Language

Honestly, I believe you need to pick the language first. Many languages like PHP have multiple frameworks available that are advisable and/or desirable to use, and this also directly impacts your productivity (real or perceived) when building out the server. This could be a hiring/staffing decision, this could be a learning decision, or this could be an efficiency decision.

If you have many people working together on a project, you want to democratize the ability to contribute. Picking a server-side language that allows the most people to be able to share the ownership of the codebase is a powerful thing, particularly when it comes to buy-in and personal investment in a product. The idea that an app *has* to be coded in a particular language because it is a particular kind of product is ludicrous.

A good developer can build anything in anything.

You may also choose a particular server-side language because of the desire to learn it. Perhaps you've decided that all the hype about Node.js needs to be explored, or perhaps you got excited about the latest release of Go and want to try Google's new runtime environment. You may be taking a step back and you're going to go with LAMP stack and PHP.

What matters is that you and everyone else that may work on this project are comfortable with the learning curve that you are signing on for with the language you choose. It could be steep, near vertical (looking at you Erlang), or almost horizontal if it's a language with which you are already familiar.

MVC Framework

I would love to be able to write this section and give you the silver bullet for which back-end framework is going to be the best for your project. I can't even definitively say that *using* an MVC framework is the best for your project. However, if you need the consistency and structure that MVC offers, then there are some obvious choices that you will find with some Googling.

I highly recommend looking at metrics like the number of stars the repo has on GitHub or the number of downloads the framework has. If I were to start listing frameworks here, then this book stops being relevant as soon as one of them falls out of common usage. When it comes to frameworks, pick a framework that is going to fulfill your needs in these key areas:

- **Routing** - Params in URLs, building out request objects for you, including the parsing of cookies and HTTP body parameters
- **View rendering** - If you're rendering views on the server-side, is there a sane syntax for interpolating data into your views? Are partials supported? Are layouts supported?
- **Data models** - Your framework doesn't have to have an ORM, but does it support data modelling of some sort? Is there middleware that allows you to bring a database connection into the framework with ease?
- **JSON** - If your framework can't handle serving up JSON/XML or some other data interchange format, you'll never be able to use it as an API.
- **Mailers** - Can your framework send e-mails natively? Can you send an e-mail when a new user registers, or requests a new authentication credential?

Libraries

Look at the list above of things that a framework should be taking care of in your application. Ask yourself how many of those are key features to the application or project you are building. Ask yourself how many you have available in your server app currently? If the answer is not all of them, then you need to source libraries that you can add into your application which will take care of some of these key aspects.

Then, ask yourself what the secret sauce of your application is. Is it a custom algorithm? Is it a mashup of API data and a clever presentation? Go back to the very beginning of this book and ask yourself what the correlation or pivot of the data is that differentiates your app. Then, ask yourself how much of it you plan on coding from scratch. Is that list long? Perhaps you should question your approach.

Are there libraries that are pre-built to take care of some of that hard work for you? Smart people do hard work on useful libraries every day. Why shouldn't you benefit from their efforts? There's a reason they were probably released open-source.

Even if it's a library or package that you're paying for, ask yourself how long it would take you to recreate all of the functionality that you're going to use. If that number of hours multiplied by your average billing rate is more than what you are going to pay for that library, then you're saving yourself money.

Also, when it comes to both frameworks and libraries, it cannot be emphasized enough how important it is to talk to other developers who may have used them. Ask around on message boards, at meetups, at conferences, even if you end up going old-school and finding online forums like IRC. Find out whehther they felt productive.

Don't ask:

- Hey, is <framework/library> cool?
- What did you think of <framework/library>?
- Is <framework/library> helpful?

Ask:

- Did you feel productive when you used <framework/library>?
- Did <framework/library> help you deliver the project, or did you deliver in spite of it?
- How much did you rely on the documentation?

Front-end Frameworks

In the world of application design, front-end frameworks have become a staple of best practice in design and architecture. They can be immensely helpful when it comes to creating interfaces that respond quickly and intuitively to user interaction. However, by necessity they do require certain concessions and compromises from the developer. Choosing to implement a front-end framework in your application can be a great decision. Or it can unnecessary complexity when you are chasing some level of credibility or a false idea that the type of app you are building can "only" be done with a front-end framework.

If you are choosing to use a front-end framework for the specific purpose of building your skills with that technology, then you are making a great decision. If you are choosing to use a front-end framework because you think it's going to make you 'cool' or somehow more credible as a developer, then I would rethink your technology choices.

With a front-end framework, you will likely be duplicating your data models, on both the front-end and back-end sides of your application. As well, most of your business logic is now going to be in the front-end of your application instead of the back-end. Also, the learning curve for most front-end frameworks the first time you use them is nearly vertical.

It's also worth noting that with front-end frameworks, there is often a myth that X has to go with Y, when it comes to pairing front and back-end frameworks. Your front-end framework is ignorant and truly apathetic about what is running on the back-end. It needs to be able to request data, and get it. If it can't do that, it doesn't matter whether your back-end is running PHP, C#, or ParseServer. Serve up JSON, have sane data endpoints, and you can pair up any back-end and and front-end you want.

UI Frameworks

One of the hardest decisions you have to make as a developer when choosing technologies is the framework that will comprise your UI. There are rare cases where building it from scratch is the right way to go. Perhaps this is your project where you intend to innovate something new in the UI world. Perhaps there is such a custom and unique set of UI components you're going to be using that doing a custom build is the way to go.

However, more often than not, you're going to want to bring in a pre-built set of UI components and layout tools to assist you in the construction of your application. Grid-based frameworks, icon frameworks, or frameworks that provide tools like modals and button stylings and other interactive components are incredibly powerful and useful tools that you have to choose.

If you haven't done any design for your application yet, you may want to wait until you have figured out what the UI challenges of the application are going to be. You may also know ahead of time that you are choosing to use a particular framework because you want to acquire significant skills in it as a result of this project. Regardless of your commitment level to a particular UI framework, understand that the reason they exist is to save you time and effort and allow you to focus on the important parts of your app, namely the features that will directly benefit the user.

ROUTES

Unfortunately, you're still not ready to code. We're getting closer, though.

Normally, when we talk about routes, we are talking about the unique combination of an HTTP verb and a path in a web application. In a desktop app or a mobile application, this doesn't necessarily have the same meaning. However, we can use the same mentality to approach each of the major "pages" or "views" that are going to exist in our application. There is a necessity to plan out the various paths that our users are going to take through our application. If we are building an API, what are the endpoints that are going to give users access to the data which we are offering?

It may sound like the flogging of a dead horse, but go back to your User Specifications. Given the following spec:

As a **user,**

I want to search for **stories** that I find interesting,

Because I like new content.

Given that I am on the search page,

When I enter a **keyword** to search for,

I get a listing of **stories** that match,

And I can click on a **story** to read it.

I can intuit the following routes/pages from it:

- /search - A search page that would be served up via a GET request in a web app, or loaded as a specific view in a desktop/mobile app. It would show the controls to initiate a search.
- /search?q=keyword - This is also the search page, but it includes parameters in a querystring that would trigger the production of results based on the keyword that was searched.
- /stories/:id - This is the link that would be clicked on to view the individual story, given a RESTful convention for route construction. In a web app, it would a GET request. In a desktop/mobile app this would represent the UI view that is showing the content from the relevant story fetched from the data store.

This is a set of three routings that come from just one user specification. Imagine if you went through all of your user specs and assembled a comprehensive list of all the routes that represent the pages/views your user would access in your application. This includes things like settings pages, profile update pages, and all of the aspects of your business logic that demonstrate your product's value. Given that you can associate the list of routes with each user spec, you now have a checklist system to verify that you have fulfilled the responsibilities in your planning.

If data models are nouns, routes are verbs.

It is far better while still in the planning stages to realize that you need to plan more than to get deep into the building of your application, and have to break your flow by reverting back to planning mode to scope out pages and features that you hadn't considered.

DESIGN

Definitely not ready to code yet, but we are making progress.

In the ideal scenario for every developer, there is some brilliant, gifted, efficient designer on staff who is able to create a layout and/or a mockup of the app and all of its pages, including documenting expectations for the interactions such as drop-down menus, modals, and active/selected states for all relevant items. Colours are given in hex codes, alphas are given whenever necessary, fonts are clearly labeled and where appropriate, min- and max-width measurements have been offered up. Unfortunately, that scenario almost never happens when you're a solo developer working on a side project.

In these less-than-ideal cases, it usually falls on the developer themselves to come up with their own layouts, colour schemes, and design ideas. Of course, in those cases, rarely is there a lack of inspiration. In many cases, seeing someone else's design or implementation of something is what triggered the inspiration for the project you've started. Some few developers do have the talent for design, but most of us mortals are forced to rely on the creativity of others in the visual realm.

However, it is absolutely critical that you plan out the layout and design of your site **before** you start building it. There is a quote of mine that I will give here, as it has been used with students for years and in my own practice as a developer for almost twenty years.

A wise man once said:

"Doing development without a design is like doing origami blindfolded.

Yes, you will get folded paper, it will not be a pretty crane."

In short, if you don't invest the time in planning out what you are going to build, you have no idea what you are going to build. It is just that simple. There are three very distinct parts to the process:

1. Wireframing
2. Storyboarding
3. Design

Wireframing is about creating a layout for your data. Your data is your product. The wireframe allows you to outline how that data is going to be laid out on the media you specify (screen, print, etc.). Storyboarding allows you to take the sketched out ideas for layouts and create a workflow with them, much as a film director would create a storyboard for a film or TV show they were creating.

Design, on the other hand, includes things such as the colours, fonts, and visual effects that are going to add a level of refinement and style to your product. Truthfully, wireframing and storyboarding are also part of design, but for the purposes of creating terminology for developers learning to plan out and manage their projects, design is being separated out to indicate those more aesthetic aspects. Your design process does include some level of specifying layouts, but for the most part it is about creating the visual aesthetic of your page(s). Design is critical!

If you are building a command-line application, you still have a responsibility for designing the interface with which your users will interact. Even an API should have some design thought put to it, if only for the documentation of the various endpoints. Every app you produce carries with it an element of design that is required to be managed and curated by the project leader. In this case, that's you.

Wireframes

If you haven't done wireframing before, it will seem odd at first to just be sketching out where elements are going to go instead of actually putting them there. However, there is a great value to using simple frames to represent your app's content. It allows you to work with proportions, it allows you to establish your data hierarchy on the page, and it allows you the opportunity to test some different layouts to determine what is going to be the best representation of the data you have chosen to present to the user. Data is your product, after all.

A wireframe is not about typography, it is definitely not about colour, and can't really represent animation. A wireframe can, however, demonstrate where key data elements will go on a page. And this is absolutely critical, because you need to make sure that you are demonstrating the significance and relationships of your data in a meaningful way. Go back to your user specifications and look at the *because* statement in each of the user stories. Remind yourself what the value is in each feature that you intend to deliver to your users.

Your user specs will inform what the scenarios are which you should construct using UI elements. Wireframes are that first translation from the description of an interaction in a user scenario into a UI context. You've decided that a user is going to have a slider with which to change the value of a setting. That tells you what kind of UI element to put into the wireframe. Your user is going to have a profile picture? Great. Square, oval, or round? Where on the page does it go? How big will it be in relation to the other elements on the page? Wireframing opens up your opportunity to experiment with different layouts without having to commit to writing actual code for the UI.

Wouldn't you rather decide now that the form only needs four boxes instead of ten, instead of after you have built out all ten including validations and error states? Now is the time to discover that you need more room for the title of each article in a news feed, not once you are dynamically populating the data into an already-constructed layout. Good wireframing can also reveal certain commonalities with UI structure and style that you can use to standardize the look and feel of your application by applying those styles and structures wherever relevant.

One of the big pitfalls that comes up when wireframing is the urge to fill in whitespace. Nature abhors a vacuum after all, and when we see large blocks of whitespace, we tend to get twitchy and have an urge to invent things to fill the space. This is just as dangerous as "Wouldn't it be cool if..." as a mechanism for causing scope-creep. Allow your design to be sparse and minimal to begin with. The far more important motivation is to have every data element you are planning to put into your wireframes have a clear source from your ERD and data design. You cannot invent data during wireframing. This is not where you add features you don't have and haven't planned for, unless it is a clear necessity to do so. And speaking from experience, it is far better to discover at this point in the planning that some mission-critical piece of functionality is missing or needs to be changed than to find out when you are deep into UI, controllers, and dynamically-interpolated view files.

Interactions should be wireframed as well. If you're going to have an auto-complete or custom drop-down menu, you should do a version of your wireframe that is going to include that visual element. Modal windows should also be wireframed in order to determine position and proportion in relation to the page itself. Fly-out menus, tooltips, UI elements that have multiple states such as accordions or calendars, these are all elements that should have a visual treatment done in order to get an understanding of how your data is going to be treated on the page.

Every data point you plan in a wireframe must have a provenance, or source, in your ERD. Otherwise, you're inventing new data and functionality. Many developers make huge mistakes at this point in their planning. Five-star ratings systems get added, videos appear out of nowhere, and social sharing buttons become the best way to fill in empty space. Keep it simple to begin with. Be willing to release a feature-lean version of your product to start. Features can be added over time as you get traction and, most importantly, feedback. Some good questions to ask yourself when you are wireframing:

- Does my navigation scheme work with the rest of my content?
- Would a user unfamiliar with the product understand the most important data points on this page?
- Have you accounted for every bit of UI interaction a user needs with the data you have presented?

Another topic with wireframing that must be discussed is the concept of responsiveness. If you are building a web application, how will it behave on a tablet or other mobile device, such as a phone? Most likely, you will need to wireframe a version for at least one other screen size. When you do this, you need to return to the three questions above and ask yourself those questions all over again. You may also want to add some extra points to consider, such as:

- Is this data point critical to the user's understanding/use of the app in this resolution?

- How important is it that I maintain the ratio of sizes to indicate data hierarchy in a smaller resolution?
- What is the minimal functionality that my users need to get value from this application?

One last note on wireframing is that until you have built a wireframe, your data exists as a one-dimensional point. Within that point is all the thoughts, ideas, plans you have made, user stories, ERD, and libraries you have chosen to use. But it is one-dimensional. Wireframing gives it shape and form and breaks it out of the world of being a concept into being a tangible product. Now you can see spatial relationships between data points and plan where on the screen information and interactions are going to go. This is when it starts to be real.

Storyboarding

Storyboarding is the practice of visually ordering elements of a story in chronological order. It is the primary mechanic behind comic strips, and also a part of the craft of making a TV show, movie, or stage production. Scenes from the storyline are presented in chronological order, and it is the storyteller's responsibility to guide the audience from one point to the next. This helps the storyteller to plot out points of tension and relaxation, understand the flow of their story, as well as planning how crucial elements will be delivered to the audience.

This applies to the construction of software applications as well. Decide what the right workflow is for your users, and use your wireframes as the story elements to plan out how a user will progress through your application. It is far better to plan out the navigation and workflow now instead of after the app is built and you have to go and re-map links and redirections to new places. And since you are literally telling the story of the flow of data from one point of your application to another, you can actually start this process with your

User Stories by arranging them in the order in which you expect the user will interact with the data.

Now is a very critical, validating time for your application. Now is when you get to question most of your assumptions about whether it all works or not. Now is the time to correct any short-sighted mistakes about UI and data collection, identify points of friction, and think about ways to simplify your app. Simplification is hard, paradoxically. One of the hardest things you will ever do is build an app that is simple to use. Even more difficult is keeping that app simple to use. Forget that you are the one building this app for just a moment, take a step back and look at the UI you are proposing. Can you still find the value? Does it seem overly-complex, or do you realize that you have them filling in five forms when one would do? Challenge your assumptions as much as you can. Get someone who has never seen it before to look at it and tell you what they think they should do on each "page". Don't ask them if they like it, they'll tell you yes. Instead, ask them what they think that page is for and ask them which page do they think they would go to in order to perform a certain task.

Once you decide on a final chronological order, build your navigation to match. It is no coincidence that most major products' navigation order is the workflow from start to finish that they want you to take through the application or content.

Design

When I am labelling this section as Design, I am really talking about a number of smaller categories all rolled up into the process of creating the visual aesthetic of your application. These categories are elements like colours, typography, graphics, icons, and animations. There is a lot within this realm and most of it is overwhelming and daunting to most developers. There is a reason why designers have their own discipline separate from developers, and it's because of the level of training and knowledge they have to have to be competent with all of these elements. If you are reading this book, you are a developer, not a designer. Colour theory and typography are concepts you are aware of, but probably don't have a lot of experience implementing at a professional level.

The design of an application matters, absolutely. However, you're the expert on coding, not balancing hues and picking whether a serif or sans-serif font is the best. I want to offer up some general guidelines that you can use to improve the quality and presentation of your site. I also want to offer some advice as to how you can go about picking a layout and colours for your application without feeling like you're just ripping off someone else.

Themes

I once heard a quote that said, "90% of the web is plagiarized. The rest we just stole." This comes from the fact that on the web you can right-click and see the page source of any site, including its CSS and in most cases JS. With the advent of developer tools built into browsers, the ability to inspect a particular element on a page and see both the HTML and the CSS which created that layout or effect has propelled a lot of developers to far greater heights than if they had been required to re-develop all of those skills from scratch. Democratized access to innovation has elevated the entire industry, in both skill level and maturity.

One of the biggest questions when it comes to design that I hear from developers is, "Is it okay to use a theme?" The shortest answer is, yes. It is okay to use a theme. There are no Layout Police that are going to come and arrest you because your site looks like someone else's. Customizing the theme is ideal, because then you are using a pre-defined layout and style as a foundation upon which to build an identity. If there is a theme that typifies the type of app which you are building, then it makes sense to leverage pre-built structure to present your data. You used libraries and frameworks, didn't you? Why not use a theme too?

Keep in mind, there is a reason that so many startups share the same layout for their landing pages. There is a reason that most social media is blue. There is a reason that we like icons next to navigation options. These are design patterns that we have grown accustomed to, and we feel comfortable interacting with the patterns that we know.

CRAP

Contrast

Contrast focuses our attention, and highlights what the most important parts are to take away from any layout. The same way that jewellers will display their wares on dark velvet to make the precious gems and metal sparkle and catch the eye, you can use contrast in your layouts to draw the user's attention to key points such as headers, important pieces of data, or errors. There are many ways to create contrast on a page.

Visual weight can be used to create a focal point. A large hero image, a large font for a header, or a splash of colour can all focus the eye, and then as elements descend in size and intensity, the eye is pulled around the page. You can also use contrast with fills and outlines to accentuate an element by putting a contrasting colour behind it, or drawing a border or outline around it in order to emphasize it on the page.

Repetition

Repetition ties objects or images together. You can use repetition of colours, text elements, shapes, all in an effort to produce a unifying feeling to the content you are presenting. Remember that you are presenting a unique, compelling set of data which is going to benefit the user. Tie the various elements of benefit on the page together by using repeating colours, fonts, or shapes.

Alignment

Alignment indicates polish, strength, and professionalism. Text on a page is easier to read if it is properly aligned. Pages should have a natural margin and both text blocks and images should align along them. Applications tend to organize themselves naturally in rows and columns, so you should make sure that the various elements you are putting onto a page align consistently both horizontally and vertically. The same way that store shelves imply neatness and quality when their products are tidily aligned, your product will appear more professional and trustworthy if you have taken care of this small but critical aspect of the design.

Proximity

Proximity implies a connectedness within objects in a user's field of view. Placing objects close together implies their relationship and focuses the user's attention on them. This is why captions are placed in close proximity to the images which they annotate, and headings are placed near the content which they are announcing. If you are taking care to correlate your data, then you can document those correlations both with the data itself, but also by presenting them in close proximity to each other. Also, proximity is for the user's convenience. We want to save them time, so proximity allows us to group related things together to make it more efficient for the user to get value out of the product.

Summary

Overall, design matters. Whether you are starting out working from a theme and letting that inform your layouts in your wireframes or starting from wireframes and working by adding layers such as colour and typography later, it is imperative that you put time and craft into making some good, informed decisions about the appearance and interactions in your application. Wireframes may even evolve into full mockups, with colour and font included. Along with your user stories and your ERD/Data Design, this forms the backbone of your project planning.

This should not be the place where your app development dies, because you didn't have a good sense of what colours to use. There are colour palette generators out there, themes with various colour schemes. Go look at other products in your vertical and analyze what colour palettes they are using. As previously mentioned, it's hard to go wrong with blue for social media, green for anything money or finance, and yellow or orange for food. Black or white are artistic, with white usually encouraging minimalism. Think about the product you want to make, and don't let something like font choice be the reason you can't deliver a great experience.

VERSION CONTROL

You'd like to start coding now, but you're not ready yet. You need to make sure you can keep track of your project before you start building it.

Version control systems give developers the ability to keep track of their work on their projects and provide a clear, documented timeline of the milestones involved in building the product. The acronym (initialism, really) VCS for Version Control Systems is one that we never see outside of job postings, but it is an important part of the developer workflow. By far, the most popular version control tool is git. The git tool is the result of Linus Torvald's feud with BitKeeper back in 2005. Designed to be simple, lightweight, distributed, and efficient, the git tool has soared in adoption since it was released. It has become a staple of developer toolkits worldwide, and is the industry-standard version control system used by software devs.

That being said, it is consistently one of the weakest points of younger developer's workflow. And to be such a critical part of the proper professional tracking of a project, it is essential that when planning your project that it is a priority to handle this part of your development well. Whether you are using git or another competing product such as mercurial, you need to make sure that you are comfortable with the proper, professional workflow.

The other common complication with less-experienced developers on projects using version control is when you are collaborating with other developers. The workflow of version control when collaborating is one that every developer needs to internalize. Even if you are working by yourself, you want to make sure you are using excellent version control practices. There is never a point in a developer's career where having good version control workflow is going to be a disadvantage.

Good Branching Strategy

With version control systems, especially distributed systems like git and mercurial, you end up with a master branch that is intended to be the clean, working version of your product at any given point. That means that if you are doing active development on your master branch, you are violating that intention. You are corrupting the one version of your product that you can always go back to and be sure it is stable. This is why it is so important to make sure that you are using a good branching strategy on your repository.

Once you have your development environment set up (as discussed in Scaffolding), you want to commit that to your repository. That is a very specific milestone, where you know that you have all of the initial libraries and configuration done to allow you to begin working on all of the planning you have done up to this point. However, once that initial commit into your repository has been done, your very next step should be creating and switching to a branch for the first steps of feature development. Keep your development work confined to the branches, so that the iterative process of building, debugging, and refactoring your code is contained in the branch. Only when you know that you have stable code in that branch do you want to switch back to your master branch and consider merging in the new feature which has been built.

It is recommended to name your branches effectively, too. When you are working on new functionality, name your branch *feature/name-of-feature*, such as *feature/forgot-password* or *feature/upload-avatar-image*. This way, you or any other developer looking at the list of branches will clearly and quickly understand the intention of the branch and the development work within it. When you are correcting a problem in functionality, what we would normally call a bug, then name your branch accordingly. A pattern such as *bugfix/name-of-bug* is a good one to follow. Some good examples include titles like *bugfix/cannot-save-profile* or *bugfix/edit-deletes-data*.

Other prefixes you can use on branch names include *hotfix/*, *test/*, and *refactor/*. Ultimately, you should come up with a branching strategy that is right for your style of development, but build on the basic idea that your active development occurs in branches off of your master branch, and you only merge from a branch onto master when you are sure that the development work is stable and will contribute to the clean, working version of your product.

Collaboration

Collaboration when using version control can be one of the most rewarding experiences as a developer. Seeing work being done asynchronously, watching features just come in and contribute to the overall health of the product, even just getting access to some piece of code that another dev has written that is going to make your task easier, these are all ways in which collaborating with other developers can be rewarding. Even if you are the sole developer on a product, you may need to collaborate on it with yourself, from working on the project on multiple workstations.

Merge conflicts, where the same line of code in a file has been edited in more than one repository, happen. Sometimes it occurs even despite our best intentions, but they do happen. We can minimize the number of them that happen by following good collaboration habits. This will also minimize the impact of them when they do occur, so that even if they do disrupt functionality, the footprint of the disruption should be minimal. Part of the collaboration strategy relies on the aforementioned role of the master branch in your product's development. If all developers on the team are keeping the master branch clean and functional, then when master branches from multiple distributed repositories are merged, there should be few problems. Those that do occur should have a small footprint.

Using the git paradigm, here is a workflow that all collaborators can follow to minimize the number of disruptions:

1. Repository begins with git init or git clone. Remote repositories are linked up manually or automatically.

2. Scaffolding occurs, where the development environment is configured for use.

3. git branch (or git checkout -b) is used to create a new branch for development purposes.

4. Active development is done on the branch. Debugging, testing, files added/removed.

5. Development finishes, the work is tested (still on the branch) for stability, efficiency, and accuracy.

6. git checkout master - This will change to the timeline of the master branch, reflecting the clean, working version of the product.

7. git pull remote master - Remote will probably be named 'origin', if following the git conventions. However, you could be pulling from some other remote such as another developer workstation, a staging server, or an internal private git repository for your company/team. The importance of doing this before you merge is to integrate the work of your co-workers into your local repository before you add the result of your development in.

8. Test the product, before you merge. Your colleagues have the best of intentions, just as you do. However, they are also only human.

Make sure the build of your app has not been compromised with the new code. You shouldn't be moving ahead with the merging of your feature in if there is a problem. This is the one case where master may not be a working version of your product, and anytime that is the case it is worth stopping development and resolving this issue.

9. git merge category/my-branch-name - Assuming that master is working, or brought to a working state, this is going to merge your code from your recently completed development onto the master branch.

10. Test again - You just changed master, so test it. Make sure it's working, stable, efficient, before you push it off of your computer and to any other place for consumption. Make sure you didn't break the build either.

11. git push remote master - Now that you know that master is a clean, working version of your product (or have made it that way through debugging and continued iteration), share it with all other collaborators for their consumption. Ideally, they are following the same workflow as you.

It is worth noting that where the merges happen above that the workflow could be changed out to use pull requests instead, and be just as valid. The point being that there is always a careful consideration for maintaining the sanctity of the master branch, and testing it each time changes are made to its timeline before continuing on with any further changes to your own master branch or anyone else's.

Last, but not least, I just want to ask all of you reading this book a personal favour. If you have liked even one thing out of here, if even one piece of advice has made you a better developer, then do me this one small favour:

Don't code on master.

SCAFFOLDING

The good news is, you're almost ready to code. You're at that fingers-over-the-keys point, itching to get started.

What you need to do now is go through a process called 'Scaffolding', where you establish the basis for your dev environment. This is a critical time, where you are doing a little bit of setup, and a lot of architecture for the specific purpose of giving yourself a solid base from which to work. Scaffolding involves getting the initial configuration done for your application, so that any of the third-party libraries and frameworks you are choosing to include are set up to work together. This allows you to have the basis you can work from to build in the business level and appearance of your application.

Especially if you are going to be working with a web application or a hybrid mobile application, there are a number of key steps you're going to want to go through. At a structural level, you need to do the following things:

Set up version control

We'll talk a lot more about version control in the next section of the book, but you're going to want to set up a repository to track the progress of your project. Without question, git is going to be the tool of choice, but if you are more comfortable with SVN or Mercurial, use whatever is going to work the best for you. Tools should be a partnership, not a negotiation. However, the key piece here is that you're going to want to do it, and do it properly. With all of your scaffolding steps, it's imperative that you are not just paying lip service. These are steps that will make or break the initial development you're going to do. It's a favour to yourself to do them properly.

Download/Install all resources

Whether you are using a framework, whether you have any third-party libraries or packages that you're going to be including, you need to set up the initial files from which you will be building. If you're using a web framework like Rails, Meteor, or Django, you've got a command-line generator command which you can use to initialize the set of files which get your project started. From there, you'd want to use your package management tools, like bundler for Rails, atmophere/npm for Meteor, or pip for Django to take your app to the next level by installing the third-party libraries and helpers you will need to craft your business logic.

Perhaps you're building in some other language, such as PHP, or using a framework like Sinatra, Flask, or Express to build your application. Some of those have generators, but in the most common of cases you're going to be creating a set of files and building out your directory structure manually. From there, again there may or may not be a package manager to help you and it may be up to you to make sure that packages and libraries are effectively and accurately included in your application's structure.

Use CDN links whenever possible

Particularly with libraries like Bootstrap or Foundation, plugins, Java-Script libraries such as jQuery or Angular, you want to make sure that you are using CDN links whenever possible. That is giving your app the best chance of leveraging cached copies of these libraries on your users' machines for better performance. This is absolutely a best practice, and can dramatically decrease the initial load time of your app for your users.

Make sure the app starts

One of the biggest mistakes I see young developers make is to start coding on a bad foundation. I worked in restaurants for many years, and one of the lessons you learn when you work in food service is that if you have a half pot of old coffee and a half pot of fresh coffee, you don't combine them. You end up with a full pot of old coffee, and no one wants that. The same principle goes for code. If you have a broken project, and you write great code based on it, you still have a broken project. When you get done installing and configuring the frameworks and libraries you intend to use, make sure your app starts and you get the basic welcome page or default functionality you would expect. If it doesn't, fix that before you start on any of the tasks you have outlined to build your application.

When you get to the front-end work on your project, there are a number of things you can do to make sure that the work you did during the Design phase is realized to its fullest extent:

Start with static layout first

This is another huge pitfall and mistake that I see made all the time. Starting off trying to make your layout from a disconnected set of views, partials, and layouts is like trying to serve a dinner party for four on a table you haven't assembled yet. Always start off building out your front-end using a static layout. Use your CDN links or included script and style files in your layout, and build out using placeholder content to make sure that your layout and styling are going to work. Solve the problems here in your styling, because if it doesn't work with a static version, it is never going to work when you start trying to pump dynamic content into it. Additionally, once you have your static layout finalized, you can easily cut and paste it into views, partials, and layouts.

Use placeholder services to provide both images and text

Image placeholder services like PlaceKitten, LoremPixel, UnsplashIt, and FillMurray are great ways to provide sample image content into your application at whatever size you want. All you have to do is properly construct a URL which usually falls in the format of http://service.com/width/height in your image tags to be able to have their service provide you with a sample image.

When it comes to text, there are dozens of text generators, all variations on the original Lorem Ipsum text used by typesetters to replicate the flow and feel of real text without having the responsibility of typing it all out yourself. Some of them are somewhat famous, such as Bacon Ipsum, Hipster Ipsum, and Samuel L. Jack-sum. It doesn't matter which one you use, what matters is that you are getting a representative quantity of text for each layout element on the page.

Solve layout problems now, not later

Developers especially, but humans in general, have a confirmation bias when we build something. We know what it will do, where the weak points are, and we tend to avoid doing anything that might compromise our creation. We get emotionally attached to our work, and that causes us to only ever use it in "good" ways, never stress-testing it. With a web layout, and especially with a layout that is going to be subject to user-generated content, you have a responsibility to try and break your layout.

You have a title, that you expect will be about 60-70 characters in length. What happens when you put 250 characters in it? Or 12? Does your layout stand up to the rigours of bad data? If it doesn't, you need to address the shortcomings now with CSS or more semantic HTML. Test your image sizes, your text lengths, string lengths in input fields. It is far better to figure out that something might be a problem now and fix it, rather than finding out after you have launched and you have customers complaining about the poor performance of your product.

Use the CLI/REPL to test queries and methods

When working on the back-end of your application, I always recommend starting with your database models first. Make sure you can effectively and consistently query data from your tables and populate your relationships the way you want to before you start trying to build that business logic into your actual application. Load up the REPL (Read-Eval-Print-Loop environment) for your language, require in your modules and db connection libraries, and test your queries there. As has been said in many other areas of this book, it's far better to figure out that a query isn't working well now rather than when you already have significant infrastructure committed.

Code atomically

Anytime you've done a piece of code twice, convert it into a function. As soon as your methods start growing monolithic in size (> 10-12 lines), break the tasks up into smaller functions. Break your functionality down into its atomic parts and make sure that you understand the flow of data from one to the other. It also makes your code more testable, more maintainable, more re-usable. Methods and modules should follow the **FIRST** principle:

F - Fast

I - Independent

R - Re-usable

S - Simple

T - Testable

COMMUNICATION

You're ready to code! Get to coding! Why aren't you coding yet?

Project Management Tools

It is best practice to use a project management tool to track tasks that need to be done. Popular tools such as Trello, Pivotal Tracker, Asana, and JIRA are all excellent choices. Some are free, some are not. Many developers choose to use GitHub Issues to track their progress and especially keep track of bugs that are found. One great tool for those of you that are more GitHub focused is called ZenHub, created by AxiomZen. It is a browser extension that converts your GitHub issues board to have the appearance of Trello-like tools.

Given that many tools such as Trello and Asana are real-time now, and offer such a rich suite of tools for little or no fee, it is almost ridiculous not to be using one of these tools to keep track of your project. Create a board for your User Stories. Use the attachment feature to link your ERD files and wireframes. Colour-code your tasks according to difficulty, put labels on them for whether they are front-end, back-end, API, or database tasks. Keeping yourself organized will keep you on track. Given the plethora of free tools with rich functionality that are out there, there's no excuse for being disorganized.

Team chat tools

It should hopefully go without saying that when you are working by yourself that there are few other collaborators with which you need to communicate. However, quite often the situation will arise where you will be in a situation where you need to work with other people on your project. This could be because you have a designer on the team, because you have someone working with you and the tasks are divided up between you, or it could be because you have a client with whom you need to stay in contact.

Regardless of whether your situation is outlined above, or you are in a completely different scenario that requires you to communicate in order to complete your project, communication is critical. Even when I am working by myself on something, I find that I am still "communicating" with myself, even if it is in the form of notes left in an idea notebook, comments left in code, git commit messages, or thoughts I have added to a project management tool. Success is all about managing expectations. It is better to underpromise and overdeliver.

In addition to project management tools, there are many communication tools available. Instant messengers abound, all real-time tools that can be used to exchange messages with teammates. Slack, Flock, Telegram, HipChat, WhatsApp, Skype, IRC, and Hangouts, just to name a few. Each has their benefits and disadvantages. All of them have a certain level of service that they provide for free for teams, and then if you have the budget to be able to pay a per-user or per-team fee, you can enjoy a luxurious addition of other features that will hopefully boost your productivity enough to justify the expense. A quick web search will show you that there are plenty of opinions about which one is better, which one is cheaper, which has the Cool Kids™ on it, etc. What matters isn't which tool you use, what matters is that you are using one when you are in need of team communication. For a distributed team, communication tools like this are absolutely imperative. I know of teams which are distributed all over the world that use tools like Skype so that they can have an open video stream going on with all the team members all day long.

Things that should be communicated between team members are what tasks are being worked on, ideas about implementations, conversations about the best way to approach a problem, links to tutorials for any new technologies which are being included in the project, and any static assets (images, audio files, etc) which a team member has created or acquired to contribute to the project.

While many people have strong opinions about being digitally tethered to their mobile devices and where divisions of responsibility and availability are, I do recommend using a mobile client for whichever team communication tool you choose to use. The situation where the team is meeting and a member is late due to transit issues or something like that will occur. Being able to drop a quick message in the chat to say, "Hey, I'll be a few minutes late." is invaluable. It allows you to remain accountable to your team.

Accountability

One of the biggest mistakes that teams make on a regular basis is forgetting to be accountable to each other. The entire team is responsible for the delivery of the product, regardless of which tasks a particular team member has been assigned. Even if your teammates are your friends, it is expected and professional to hold them accountable for delivery of the tasks to which they have been assigned. And conversely, they should be holding you accountable for your deliverables at the same time. This is another part of the expectation-setting that I referenced before. It's critical that as a team you can stay in communication, so that each team member can be relied on to deliver when they have promised to do so.

TECHNICAL DEBT

Every product contains some degree of technical debt. There are many definitions of technical debt online, but I will broadly define it here as *development work that you chose not to finish before shipping your product*. This definition of *technical debt* is using the term *finished* in the context of the glossary in the section above. There are many reasons that technical debt may exist. The most common reasons are both regrettable. These are:

1. The dev team runs out of time for refactoring and optimization before delivering the final product.
2. The dev team elects to not refactor or improve code.
3. The dev team chooses a third-party solution that is not ideal, but functional, instead of writing their own implementation.

All of these reasons are regrettable because they are a demonstration of **poor project planning.** With proper scoping, proper planning beforehand, and a clear focus, none of these reasons should ever exist.

There are other less regrettable reasons for technical debt, including (but not limited to):

1. A feature is changed after being developed, leaving vestigial (unnecessary) code behind.
2. Staffing on a dev team changes mid-project and a new approach to developing a feature is taken by replacement staff.
3. A partial and/or naive implementation of a feature is all that is called for, as the feature will be listed as 'Beta' or some other expectation set for a less-than-stellar experience.
4. There was no testing done. (Note: This is regrettable, but may not be a decision for which the developer is responsible.)

One of the challenges that every team and every individual developer will have is deciding on what "done" means in terms of the code, and the product. How much technical debt can you justify leaving in a product when it is deployed? What is the limit of your professional ethics which decides when you are willing to put your name on a product and declare your contributions "good enough" for deployment? That is a question that no book can answer adequately. What I can say is that as a professional, you will forever be chasing a point where not only is there no distance between 'I have been presented with a problem' and 'I know the solution', but the code you write for the solution carries no technical debt with it. That point is forever in the future, because there will always be another opinion about how to do what you want to do. Code can always be refactored, improved, extended, or rewritten.

There are products in the market which have the most beautiful, well-written and well-refactored code imaginable. And they may or may not be successful. And there are definitely products used every day with criminal amounts of technical debt in the codebase. Where is your balance between *done* and *deployable*?

CHEATSHEETS

Principles of Project Planning

1. No one hires you to code.
2. Your data **is** your product.
3. User stories are your foundation.
4. Test your code.
5. Store your data the way you intend to query your data.
6. Data models are nouns, routes are verbs.
7. Data doesn't have to be ugly.
8. Until you wireframe, your product is one-dimensional.
9. Don't code on master.
10. Start with static pages first.
11. Your deadlines decide when the development is done.
12. There is no excuse for poor communication on a product team.
13. Assume that all data coming into your app is tainted.

Starting a git repository

mkdir myproject cd myproject git init touch README.md git add README.md git commit m "Initial commit"

Standard git workflow

git checkout -b feature/<newfeature>

<code>

<commit frequently>

<test that your code works>

git checkout master

git pull origin master

<resolve any conflicts>

<test that your code works>

git merge feature/<newfeature>

<resolve any conflicts>

<test that your code works>

git push origin master

www.ingramcontent.com/pod-product-compliance
Lightning Source LLC
Chambersburg PA
CBHW031229050326
40689CB00009B/1522